KNOWLEDGE ENCYCLOPEDIA

REPTILES & AMPHIBIANS

© Wonder House Books 2024

All rights reserved. No part of this book may be reproduced or transmitted in any form by any means, electronic or mechanical, including photocopying and recording, or by any information storage and retrieval system except as may be expressly permitted in writing by the publisher.

(An imprint of Prakash Books)

contact@wonderhousebooks.com

Disclaimer: The information contained in this encyclopedia has been collated with inputs from subject experts. All information contained herein is true to the best of the Publisher's knowledge.

ISBN : 9789354400018

Table of Contents

Unique Creatures	3
Evolution of Amphibians	4–5
Characteristics of Amphibians	6–7
Evolution of Reptiles	8–9
Reptilian Features	10–11
Orderly Amphibians	12
The Class Reptilia	13
Newts and Salamanders	14
A Tad of a Journey	15
Frogs and Toads	16–17
Turtle or Tortoise?	18
Alike but Unlike	19
Crawling Crocodilians	20–21
The World of Snakes	22
A King Among Snakes	23
The Giant of Galapagos	24–25
Sensitive Amphibians	26
The Venomous Black Mamba	27
Activate Defence Mode	28–29
Home Is Where the Habitat Is	30–31
Word Check	32

UNIQUE CREATURES

Amphibians and reptiles are related to each other. Reptiles actually evolved from amphibians. The ferocious crocodile, the slithering snake, the slow tortoise, and the colour-changing chameleon are all classified as reptiles. Even the mighty dinosaurs belong to the same group.

To understand reptiles, we need to go back in time—not just a few thousand years—but more than 300 million years, when a branch of **amphibians** evolved into reptiles.

But what are amphibians? The word 'amphibian' combines the Greek words for 'both' and 'life', denoting that these creatures live on land and in water. Most amphibians have lungs and also breathe through their skin. They need to keep their skin wet in order to absorb oxygen, so they secrete a type of mucous that keeps it moist.

◀ Frogs are amphibians as they spend parts of their lives on land and in water

▶ Although an alligator is a reptile, it can swim well in water and crawl on land

Evolution of Amphibians

The fossil record of amphibians has been poor until recently. However, new discoveries give us a clear picture of the history of amphibians. As the Silurian Period went on, the diverse species of fish continued to evolve. Scientists do not know for certain if they got tired of fighting off too many predators or if they had too much competition for food, but eventually some fish began to move towards land.

The Missing Pieces

The first animals to move to land and settle there were the arthropods. They had started their journey towards land 100 million years ago. The bodies of these animals were uniquely adapted to life on land as they had strong legs, light bodies, and hard **exoskeletons** that helped them conserve water.

These animals had to figure out how to conserve water, move, stay safe from predators, exchange gases (like oxygen and carbon dioxide), and learn to support themselves against the strong pull of gravity.

▲ An extinct relative of the modern scorpion, called Slimonia, was one of the earliest animals to live on land along with mites and spiders

The Story Begins

During the Devonian Period, land was occupied by arthropods and **tetrapods**. It is said the amphibians evolved from tetrapods and were related to the primitive **lobe-finned fish**. These fish probably had lungs that helped them breathe on land. Their bony limbs had digits at the ends that helped them crawl on land.

Eusthenopteron is a fossil belonging to the late Devonian Period. Scientists believe this animal was near the main line of evolution from fish to amphibians. It was about six feet long, had a broad skull with teeth, and was a carnivore. The vertebral column was not well developed, but the fins had bony structures for support.

Eusthenopteron was not built for life on land. It probably lived in shallow waters, climbing small rocks and plants in search of food.

▲ A beautifully preserved fossil of Eusthenopteron

💡 Isn't It Amazing!

In the Late Triassic Period, amphibians reached gigantic proportions. There lived a giant salamander called *Metoposaurus algarvensis*. It was the size of a small car and perhaps even ate small dinosaurs!

Paving the Path

The fossil of an aquatic animal called *Tiktaalik roseae* was discovered in 2004 in Canada. It was a tetrapod and about nine feet long. It had sharp teeth and, unlike fish, it could move its head from side to side to look for prey and predators. It probably had arms with elbows, wrists, and shoulders. Hence, it is considered to be the first fish with limbs. It had a flat skull with bulging eyes like that of a modern crocodile, suggesting it swam beneath waters in lakes, streams, and swamps.

▶ An illustration of the Tiktaalik roseae

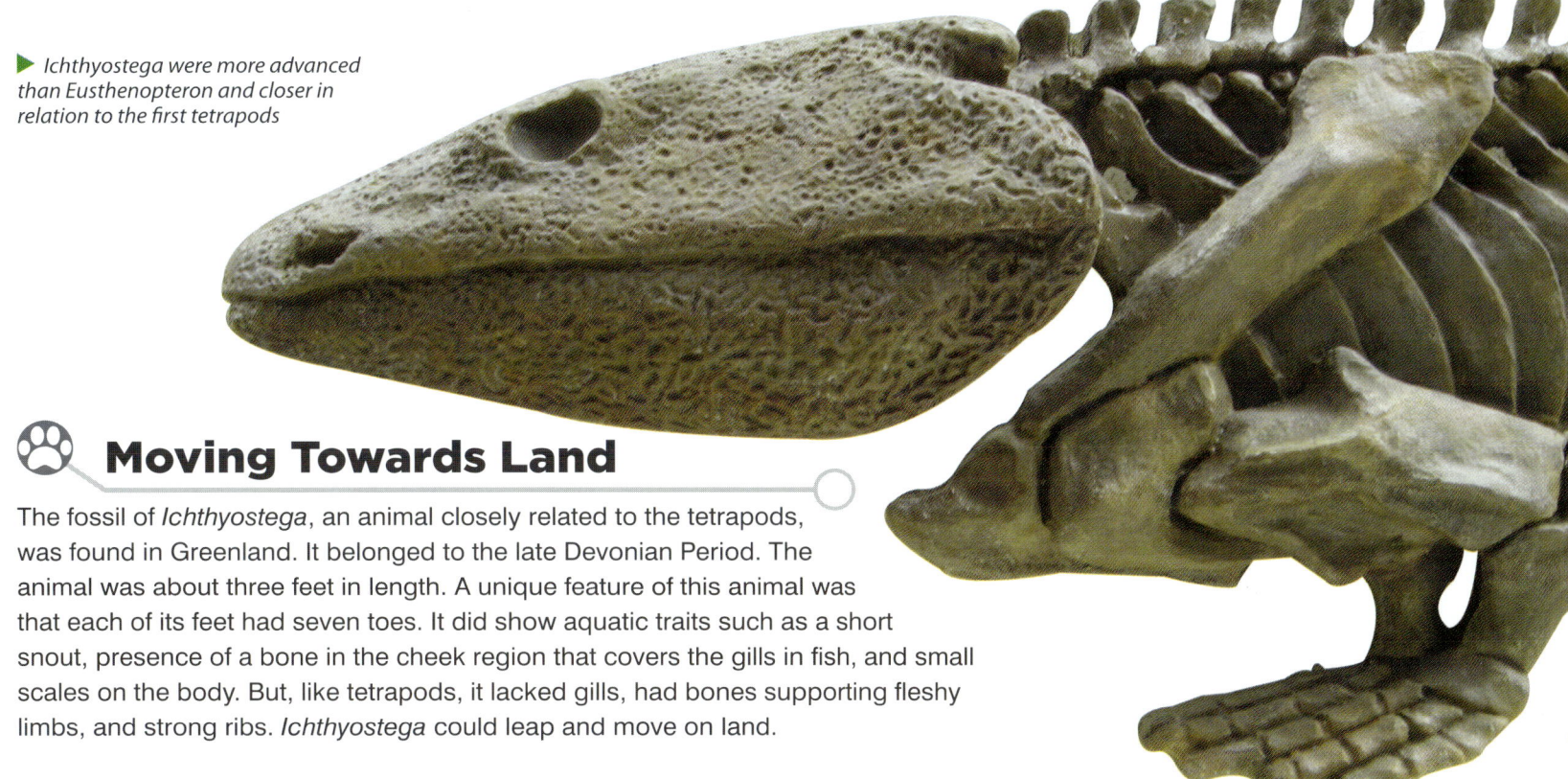

▶ *Ichthyostega were more advanced than Eusthenopteron and closer in relation to the first tetrapods*

🐾 Moving Towards Land

The fossil of *Ichthyostega*, an animal closely related to the tetrapods, was found in Greenland. It belonged to the late Devonian Period. The animal was about three feet in length. A unique feature of this animal was that each of its feet had seven toes. It did show aquatic traits such as a short snout, presence of a bone in the cheek region that covers the gills in fish, and small scales on the body. But, like tetrapods, it lacked gills, had bones supporting fleshy limbs, and strong ribs. *Ichthyostega* could leap and move on land.

🐾 Landed

About 340 million years ago, the evolution of the first known family of amphibians took place. They were called the *temnospondyls*. *Eryops* is an example of this group. It had a stout body, large skull, and a strong vertebral column, suggesting the animal could move on land. Its teeth were sharp, indicating that it could have been a carnivore.

▲ *Being short with broad limbs might have helped the Eryops walk on land*

🐾 What Happened to Ancient Amphibians?

Ancient amphibians were one of the largest predators on land for millions of years. But in the Permian Period, about 280 million years ago, Earth's climate changed. This period marks the largest mass extinction in Earth's history. Wetlands and swamps were replaced by vast deserts. But amphibians needed water to reproduce and survive. The change in climate caused many of the amphibian species to die out.

🐾 Extinction and Resurgence

The Permian Mass Extinction was an event which wiped out more than 95 per cent of all life on Earth. This included the giant amphibian predators. However, a few survived in the shadows of the reptiles (dinosaurs).

During the Jurassic Period, the climate changed once again, giving rise to wetlands, and the surviving amphibians evolved to form the modern amphibians we know today, such as frogs, salamanders, and newts.

🏅 Incredible Individuals

Jodi Rowley is a biologist who studies amphibians, focusing on their diversity, environment and the threats to their existence. Today, it is said that one-third of all amphibian population is threatened with extinction and Jodi Rowley is taking measures for their conservation. She is mainly focussed on the conservation of Southeast Asian amphibians.

Characteristics of Amphibians

To us human beings, from where we stand at the highest position on the evolutionary scale, amphibians seem like just another set of animals that cohabit Earth with us. But these animals, which are at the base of the evolutionary scale, have many interesting tales to tell.

The Heart of the Matter

Fish and amphibians have similar structures for many internal organs such as the stomach, gall bladder, liver, and kidney. But their hearts are structured differently. A fish has a two-chambered heart, where one chamber receives blood and the other chamber pumps blood out.

On the other hand, amphibians have a three-chambered heart. The first chamber receives the oxygenated blood, the second chamber pumps it to the entire body, and the third chamber receives deoxygenated blood.

Amphibians hearts are like balloons where they can only take up a limited amount of gas. So, they diffuse the extra oxygen through their skin.

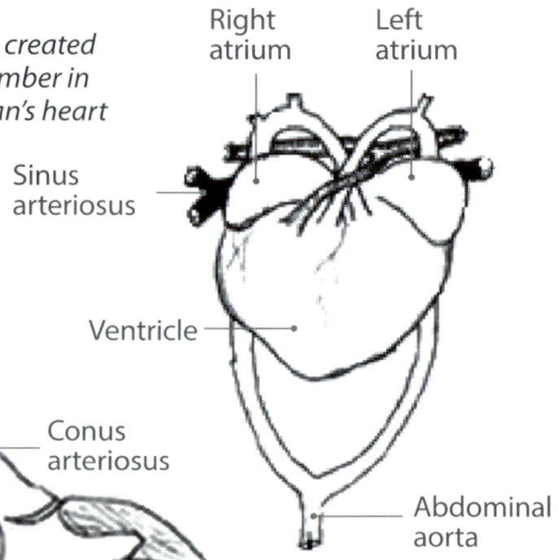

▶ Evolution created another chamber in an amphibian's heart

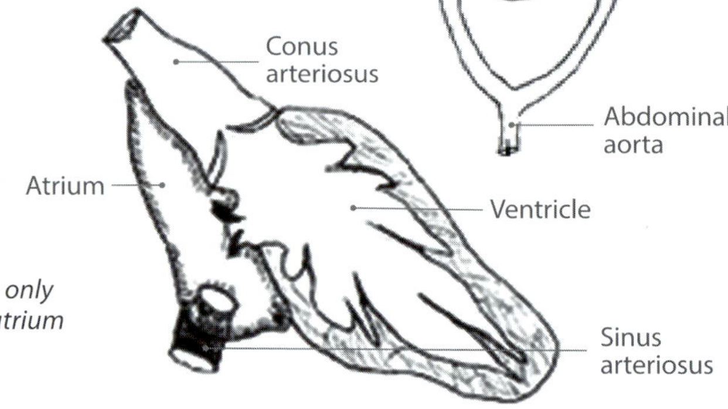

▶ A fish's heart has only two chambers: an atrium and a ventricle

Spitting Frogs

Frogs can swallow insects whole by simply pushing their sticky tongues out. The saliva helps them capture the prey. To swallow the insect, a frog closes its eyes. This helps it push the insect down towards the throat. However, when a frog eats something poisonous, it simply spits out the contents of its stomach.

Yes, you read that right, the food in a frog's stomach can come out entirely through its mouth to discard the disagreeable contents. When a frog eats bombardier beetles, the insect might squirt boiling chemicals into the frog's stomach as a defence, so the frog will spit it out.

▼ The saliva on the long, sticky tongue of a frog acts as glue for the insects

The Blind Dragon

The olm is a blind salamander that lives in caves. It resorts to its other sensory organs to hunt for food. It has pale pink skin. It does not grow, instead it maintains its red feathery gills that form when it is a **larva**, even after it reaches maturity. It was once called a baby dragon because of the small size of its snake-like body. Olm salamanders can live for more than a hundred years.

The olm salamanders have existed for nearly 20 million years in the caves of Croatia and Slovenia, but chemical pollutants are now threatening the ancient animal's existence.

▲ Olm salamanders eat crabs, snails and small insects

Most Moist

Amphibians have a moist, slimy skin as seen in most frogs. This is one of the reasons amphibians stay near water. Few amphibians live in hostile environs, such as the African bullfrogs who endure the hot, harsh climate of southern Africa. They have skins with long ridges to prevent moisture loss.

Commonly seen in amphibians is the process of metamorphosis. As the immature larva develops, it undergoes bodily changes that make it distinct from the adult it grows into. For example, most amphibians spend the early years of their lives in water, but as adults they take to land.

▲ Have you ever seen a frog look dry? They always have slimy and moist skin as they need to stay moist for survival

◀ A close-up of the larva that frogs develop from

To Catch a Fly

Research shows that frogs might have special spit that helps them catch flies. Their saliva is sticky, so frogs can extend their tongues and hold onto the flies that they catch. Their saliva, which is normally thick, liquefies to spread over the insect's body and then thickens again, effectively trapping it.

▲ Once the insect is in their mouth, frogs use their eyeballs to swallow it. The eyeballs move to the mouth cavity and push down the food, exerting force that liquifies the saliva and releases the insect

🏅 Incredible Individuals

In the 17th century, a woman named Catharina Geisslerin in Germany claimed that she had swallowed tadpoles from a swamp. She claimed that these tadpoles were happily living in her body as frogs. She also claimed that drinking milk caused these frogs to jump out of her mouth. Surprisingly, she managed to duplicitously convince physicians that this was true by vomiting frogs in front of them.

Evolution of Reptiles

The reptiles that we see on Earth today can be traced back to small lizards. These lizards roamed the planet more than 350 million years ago. They laid amniotic eggs which allowed them to move from water to land. Slowly, these land vertebrates grew in size.

320 Million Years Ago

The reptiles separated into two groups—**synapsids** and **sauropsids**. Synapsids were the early ancestors of modern mammals. Sauropsids evolved into modern birds, reptiles and dinosaurs. Though both were vertebrates, for a few million years, the synapsids became the dominant species. *Hylonomus* and *Paleothyris* were the earliest reptiles.

▲ *Hylonomus* were small, preferred to live in swamps and fed on insects

245 Million Years Ago

The Permian Mass Extinction occurred over 252 million years ago and lasted for nearly 15 million years. It wiped out 95 per cent of marine animals and 70 per cent of land animals, including most synapsids. However, the sauropsids survived and even thrived while the synapsids declined in number. This came to be known as the **Triassic takeover**.

The Mesozoic Era

Large dinosaurs gradually evolved from sauropsids nearly 225 million years ago. They dominated the land and became one of the most important groups of animals of the **Mesozoic Era**. This era was divided into the Triassic Period, the Jurassic Period, and the Cretaceous Period.

During the Triassic Period, both dinosaurs and reptiles evolved rapidly, but it is only during the Jurassic Period that the diversity of the dinosaur species evolved. Many dinosaurs became extinct towards the end of the Mesozoic Era, but the reptiles survived.

230 Million Years Ago

Evolving from their small lizard-like ancestors, reptiles began to rule not only on land but also in air. The major predators of this time were the Archosaurs. They were ancestors of the present-day crocodiles but were very different in appearance. Most animals belonging to this species had strong forelimbs and long hind legs. They had two skull openings, one in the snout and another in the lower jaw. But the function of these openings is unknown.

▼ *Proterosuchus* was the first template for the modern crocodile. It had a slight downward curve in the upper jaw

▶ Archosaur means the 'ruling reptile'. They were divided into the Pseudosuchia (crocodiles) and the Ornithosuchia (birds)

ANIMALS | AMPHIBIANS AND REPTILES

The Flying Reptiles

Pterosaurs, or 'flying reptiles', ruled the skies for about 150 million years. They should not be confused with dinosaurs, but they did belong to the group of archosaurs. They had no competition till the birds arrived millions of years later, as they were the first flying vertebrates.

Pterosaurs had light, hollow bones and their wing surface was formed by a membrane of skin similar to that of the modern bats. This membrane stretched across their thin fingers. Another membrane stretched from the wrist to their shoulder. This allowed them to fly with ease. They had small, sharp needle-like teeth in their jaws with which they could catch fish while still in flight.

▲ Archelons were about 12 feet in length

▲ Some scientists believe pterosaurs walked on their hind legs, while others believe they walked on all fours with their wings folded by their sides

▼ Sarcosuchus fossils show that the gigantic animal might have spanned 10–12 metres and weighed around 8 metric tons

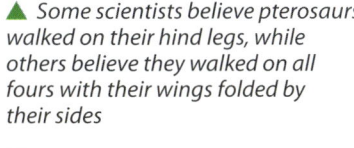

Dominating the Seas

In the oceans, marine reptiles had become the dominant species. The long-necked Elasmosaurus was one of the largest sea creatures that had needle-like teeth perfectly suited for catching fast-moving fish. The first turtles evolved during the Cretaceous Period. The Late Cretaceous Period had turtles called Archelons. They protected themselves from predators with shells that were similar to those of the modern sea turtles. They moved in the water by pushing themselves forward with their front feet. Archelon died out with the dinosaurs around 65 million years ago.

Evolution Continues

Crocodiles and lizards continued to survive and evolve alongside dinosaurs. The crocodiles grew to extremely large sizes, such as the Sarcosuchus which preyed on some species of dinosaurs. These monstrous crocodiles died out with the dinosaurs.

Some lizards lost their legs and became the first snakes. These snakes were mostly constrictors, like the modern pythons, but smaller. At some point during the evolution process, the 'Sonic hedgehog' gene switched off in snakes. This gene is necessary for the growth of limbs, and gets its name from the spines that grow from the embryo during the limb-development stage. So, snakes became limbless reptiles. However, a genetic mutation could cause them to grow limbs once again.

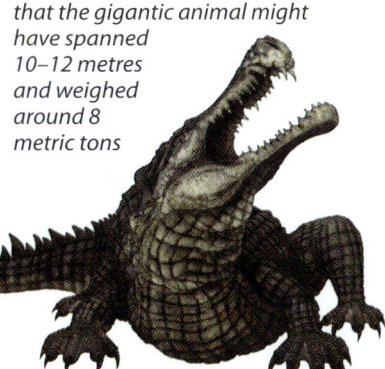

◀ While most were small, the Titanoboa is the largest known member of the serpent family. They lived near the end of the Cretaceous Period, and weighed around 1,135 kilograms, and had a length of roughly 13 metres!

Reptilian Features

The word 'reptile' refers to the animals' creeping and crawling movement. Reptiles are vertebrates, which means they have backbones which support and give shape to their bodies. They live in hot deserts, swamps, oceans, and forests. Animals can only be classified as reptiles if they possess certain characteristic features.

Cold-blooded

Reptiles are ectothermic or cold-blooded animals. Like amphibians and fish, reptiles cannot regulate their body temperature. They need sunlight and shade too. That is why, in their natural habitats, chameleons have been observed basking on hillside rocks in winters. Since they are cold-blooded, reptiles cannot survive without heat.

They lie perpendicular to the Sun, so that they can absorb a lot of sunlight. If it gets too hot, the reptile will lie parallel to the Sun or look for a shady spot. A chameleon will lighten the colour of its skin if it gets too hot, a crocodile might keep its mouth wide open, while a snake might burrow into the soil.

Reptiles in the desert region, such as Gila monsters, are nocturnal in summers because their bodies cannot handle the harsh heat during the day. However, if the temperature is tolerable, they can be diurnal.

Tough Skin

Having tough, scaly skin is the key to survival in reptiles. The skin not only acts as a protective covering, but also prevents loss of water, which saves it from drying up. The scales are made of keratin, the structural protein present in the hair and fingernails of human beings. The scales may be tiny—as found in dwarf geckos, or large—as seen in lizards. Even turtles have scales called scutes, which are arranged in a staggered manner. The scales on a crocodile are called armour.

Incredible Individuals

Back in 1992, Steve Irwin filmed a documentary with his wife, Terri Raines, called *The Crocodile Hunter*. It became so popular that he was given the opportunity to film more of the documentary, of which currently there are 50 episodes. 'Crocodile Hunter' became his nickname, even though he never actually hunted a crocodile. In fact, he was known for his close encounters with dangerous animals and his work with conservationists to help save the crocodiles.

▶ A turtle's shell has scutes made up of keratin. Though they act as the shell, they are built like a nail, beak, or horn

Eggs

Most reptiles lay eggs. Without the special feature of the amniotic eggs, reptiles could never have moved onto land. These types of eggs have leathery or hard shells which protect the embryo. The eggshell allows the flow of air but prevents vital fluids from leaking out. Inside the eggs, there are a series of fluid-filled membranes which help the embryo survive and develop.

▲ Like most creatures that are born in eggs, turtles also have egg teeth. They help the baby creature to break out of its shell

Eyes

Reptiles are dependent on their sharp vision to catch prey. Crocodiles have eyes specially adapted for hunting at night, while chameleons can move their eyes independent of each other. This helps them scan their surroundings for extremely tiny insects. However, snakes such as pythons and rattlesnakes have poor eyesight. They use what is called 'heat vision', which helps snakes sense the heat given off by warm-blooded creatures, through small openings in front of their eyes.

▼ Crocodilians and birds are the only surviving dinosaurians

▲ Chameleons sit patiently, waiting for their prey to come close. As soon as they see their prey, they stick out their tongues and grab it

Teeth

Reptiles have no specialised teeth such as canines, incisors or molars, like mammals do. They have a long row of conical teeth to catch and chew the prey, as seen in crocodiles and alligators. These animals either swallow the prey whole or cut it into bite-size portions before swallowing. Turtles have sharp edges on their jaws, which they use to bite off seaweed and other foods. Snakes have fangs. The number, placement and shape of teeth varies among reptiles.

In Real Life

The incubation temperature among crocodiles and some turtles, at a certain stage of development, determines the sex of the embryo. For example, in red-eared slider turtles, if eggs are incubated below 28° C, the hatchlings will be male. If the temperature is above 31° C, the hatchlings will be female, and in the temperatures between, it could be either male or female.

Orderly Amphibians

The amphibian world is made up of many orders. All are extinct, except three surviving orders, namely Gymnophiona, Anura, and Caudata.

Order Gymnophiona

It is also called order Apoda, which refers to limbless animals. Its members are known as caecilians. There are 206 known species of smooth-skinned, limbless, worm-like, burrowing amphibians in this order.

Caecilians live in humid, tropical regions around the world. They hunt using the two tentacles located near their mouths that help them sense the environment. Terrestrial caecilians eat soft-bodied creatures like earthworms, while the aquatic caecilians feed on eels, fish, and invertebrates.

▲ The name 'caecilians' is derived from the Latin word 'caecus' which means 'blind'

▼ Frogs are commonly brown, green or grey with very few colourful species

In Real Life

Ichthyophis beddomei or Beddome's caecilian is a yellow-striped worm-like amphibian found in the Western Ghats of India. It is a freshwater animal, living comfortably in the soil and in the tropical evergreen forests. It is also found in the agricultural areas of this region. If disturbed, it produces a whitish fluid and disappears into the soil.

 Order Anura

It is also called order Salientia and it consists of around 6,623 species of amphibians. Members of this group have short, broad bodies with no neck and tail. They have long powerful hindlimbs for leaping, webbed feet for swimming, and long, sticky tongues to catch insects. They have well-developed eyelids. Frogs and toads belong to this group.

 Order Caudata

Order Caudata is also called order Urodela and it consists of 740 species of amphibians. This group of amphibians have distinct heads, trunks and tails. They have weak limbs, smooth skin, and teeth present on both jaws. Newts and salamanders belong to this group.

▼ Caudata means 'tail-bearing', and predictably, the species that belong to this order have tails

Outstanding Amphibians

The *Paedophryne amauensis* holds the record of being the world's smallest known frog. As big as a housefly, it is said to be about 7.7 millimetres in length. It inhabits the rainforest floor of New Guinea but is very difficult to spot due to its size.

▶ Scientists believe that these frogs evolved to be tiny so that they could feed on little invertebrates for survival

ANIMALS | AMPHIBIANS AND REPTILES

The Class Reptilia

There are more than 10,000 species classified as reptiles. They are found in all continents except Antarctica. Scientists have further divided this class of animals into four orders, with each order having features special to that particular group; for example crocodiles are the only reptiles with a four-chambered heart.

The Four Orders

The four reptile orders are Testudinata—consisting of turtles, Crocodilia—consisting of crocodiles and alligators, Rhynchocephalia—consisting of tuataras, and Squamata—consisting of snakes and lizards.

01 Order: Testudinata

Characteristics: Bony shells cover most of these reptiles' bodies. They have rounded backs, flat bellies, no teeth and sharp jaws (for cutting food). They are egg-laying reptiles.
Habitat: They live in saltwater, freshwater, and semi-arid regions.
Examples: Musk turtles, mud turtles, and Hermann's tortoise

▲ A tortoise

02 Order: Crocodilia

Characteristics: These reptiles have sharp vision and big snouts. They use their powerful tails to swim, keeping their eyes and nostrils above the water.
Habitat: They are found in streams, lakes, rivers, and swamps.
Examples: Gharials, Nile crocodiles, and Caimans

▲ A crocodile

03 Order: Rhynchocephalia

Characteristics: Belonging to a sister group of order Squamata. There is only one surviving species called tuataras. This reptile has rows of spines running along the back of the neck and backbone. Their young display the remnants of a third eye, but this gradually gets covered by scales within a few months.
Habitat: They live in the islands off the coast of New Zealand.

04 Order: Squamata

a. (Suborder: Serpentes or Snakes)

Characteristics: These reptiles have long and slender bodies. They usually lack legs but have broad scales on the belly to allow forward movement. They do not have eyelids and ears.
Habitat: They are found in all environments where reptiles are found such as forests, mountains, and deserts.
Examples: Rattlesnakes, anacondas, king cobras, and coral snakes

▲ A cobra

▼ A garden lizard

b. (Suborder: Lacertilia or Lizards)

Characteristics: Most reptiles belonging to this suborder have four legs and a tail. They have eyelids and openings for the ears. Many lay eggs, but some give birth to the young ones.
Habitat: They are found in all environments where reptiles are found such as forests, mountains, and deserts.
Examples: Geckos, komodo dragons, iguanas, and monitor lizards

▲ It takes 9 months for tuataras to lay eggs, which then take 13 months to hatch!

Newts and Salamanders

Newts and salamanders—the words often go together. But are they the same thing? A newt is always a salamander, but not all salamanders are newts. The salamanders that live on land are called newts. Salamanders are reptiles that retain their tails even after they grow into adults. A salamander looks a little like a frog and a little like a lizard.

Mudpuppy

The mudpuppy is a salamander that is mistakenly believed to be capable of barking, hence it is also called a waterdog. This salamander has external, red gills which it grows at the larval stage and never loses, even after becoming an adult.

Mudpuppies spend their entire lives in water as they have no lungs. They live at the bottom of pools, rivers, streams, and lakes. When water dries up where they live, especially during summers, they burrow in mud until their pools fill up again.

Mudpuppies are found in abundance in the USA and parts of Canada. They hide in vegetation or behind logs and rocks, emerging at night to eat crayfish, snails, and worms. Unlike in many other species, females guard their eggs until they are hatched.

Isn't It Amazing!

The Chinese giant salamander is the world's largest amphibian. They are nearly 6 feet in length and 63 kilograms in weight. They are mud-coloured, with short limbs and long tails. They have a flattened head and lidless eyes. They are found in the rocky mountain streams and lakes of China.

▲ A Chinese giant salamander

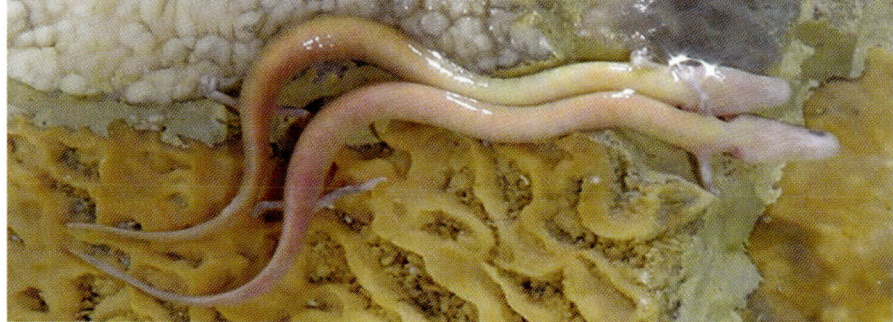

◀ A diminishing mudpuppy population can be a symptom of environmental problems in an area, as the animal is sensitive to pollutants

Kaiser's Spotted Newt

Kaiser's spotted newt is a small newt. It grows to a length of 10 or 14 centimetres as an adult. It has a black or white body dotted with stripes, and spots that are orange or red in colour. It is impossible to tell the male and female of the species apart when they are seen outside of the breeding season. During the breeding season, the male has a visibly rounded and enlarged cloacal region, while the female has a volcano-shaped cloacal region.

While most salamanders live in caves, the Kaiser's spotted newt lives in the Zagros Mountains in Iran. This is why it is also called the Iranian harlequin newt. This is surprising for a newt as most salamanders like shady and humid spots. Instead, the Kaiser's spotted newt lives in a region where water is only available for three or four months. During this period, the Kaiser's spotted newt eats a lot and finds a mate. Then, it goes underground and rests in the soil. It breathes slowly, has a low heart rate, and barely eats until water is available again.

▲ Salamanders look for moist and cool places to live in

ANIMALS | AMPHIBIANS AND REPTILES

A Tad of a Journey

Imagine an army of red-eyed tree frogs coming your way. An 'army' is what a group of red-eyed tree frogs is called. But you would only get to see the red-eyed tree frogs in person in Central America and Mexico. It inhabits tropical rainforests and likes to live near ponds and rivers.

 ### The Egg Stage

During the monsoon season, the females lay a lot of eggs on the underside of a leaf, just above a pond or a river. They might also lay the eggs in water.

The females choose the spot carefully, as the eggs need to be moist all the time. Once they lay the eggs, the males fertilise them.

The eggs of frogs do not have hard, protective shells like reptile eggs. In fact, eggs laid by frogs are quite weak in comparison. They need to be covered with water, otherwise they dry up and die. The eggs absorb the water around them and become much bigger.

 ### Hatched Eggs

After six days, when the eggs are ready to hatch, the tadpoles energetically swim around inside the egg. This energetic movement breaks the egg and releases the tadpoles. The moisture from the hatched eggs pushes the tadpoles into the pond water beneath.

The red-eyed tree frogs lay eggs that decide to hatch after carefully assessing the vibrations or signals that they pick up from their surroundings.

 ### Tadpole Stage

After hatching, the embryonic tadpoles enter a new phase of their lives. They might be able to live outside water for 20 hours, but they need to move to the water to feed on algae. They breathe with their gills and swim using their tails. Within a week, they start to develop lungs and slowly lose their tails. This marks the beginning of the metamorphosis stage of their growth cycle.

▶ *Young tadpoles*

 ### Metamorphosis

During this stage, the tadpoles begin to change into small brown froglets. This next phase is about the tadpoles developing legs. The tadpoles develop hind legs first. During this stage, the frog's head becomes distinct and the body elongates. The growth is aided by a diet of insects.

▲ *Eggs laid by red-eyed tree frog*

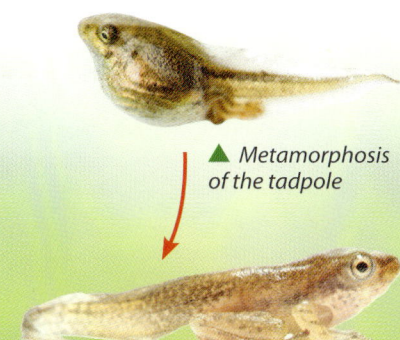

▲ *The tadpole stage of a frog*

▲ *Metamorphosis of the tadpole*

▲ *The tail is now elongated and the tadpole has visible legs*

 ### Young Adult Stage

This stage comes two or three months after birth. The tadpole is now a tiny brown froglet. Barring a tiny stub for a tail, the frog looks like an adult. At this stage, the tail is being rapidly absorbed into the body. The frog leaves the water and moves onto trees. It can survive in both water and land like all amphibians.

▼ *The green colour of the frog acts as a camouflage when it sits on leaves*

 ### Adult Stage

In the next few weeks, the frog turns green in colour. It develops blue and yellow stripes on its sides, orange feet, bluish thighs and the signature bright red eyes. It is now an adult, capable of taking care of itself and fighting its predators.

Frogs and Toads

There are around 7,411 species of frogs and toads in the world. They are found all over the world, except in Antarctica. However, they prefer warmer climatic conditions; hence, there is a greater population in the tropics. Of these, the reticulated glass frogs are especially interesting.

Reticulated Glass Frog

The reticulated glass frog is tiny—about the size of a coin—with see-through skin on its underside. If you ever get a view of the frog from underneath, you would be able to see its insides including its beating heart! The upper side is light green with spots.

The frog is found in the rainforests of Ecuador, Panama, Costa Rica, and Colombia. It eats the plants that grow along the streams in these forests. It is a nocturnal amphibian that cleverly uses its see-through underside to blend into the leaves to hide from dangerous predators.

▶ To this day, scientists cannot confirm the reason for the frog having such see-through skin on the underside of its body

Rough Males

The males of this species guard their territories fiercely. They repeatedly squeak at their predators or even other frogs who might try to trespass. If the squeaks do not scare them away, the male reticulated glass frogs wrestle them into leaving. On the other hand, if the red-eyed tree frog wants to escape a predator, it reveals its bright orange legs from underneath and bulges out its bright red eyes, shocking the predator momentarily. This gives the red-eyed tree frog a chance to escape quickly.

Colourful Leaps

Red-eyed tree frogs have suction-cup toes which help them attach to the underside of the leaves where they rest during daytime. At night, these frogs feed on crickets, moths, grasshoppers, and smaller frogs. Interestingly, unlike many other frog species which lay eggs directly in the water, the red-eyed tree frog lays them on a leaf.

▼ Reticulated glass frogs are carnivorous and feed on different kinds of insects for survival

▶ Red-eyed tree frogs have small tadpoles that need to feed on insects to survive and grow. They grow into brown froglets, and only turn green as adults

Responsible Fathers

Red-eyed tree frog females lay eggs on the underside of the leaves. The bunch of eggs they lay at once is called a 'clutch' and these eggs stick on the leaves because of a jelly-like substance.

Then, the males guard the eggs until they are hatched. They protect the eggs from wasps who might come to eat the eggs. The spotted green upper side of the frog resembles the cluster of eggs it is trying to protect. This camouflage pattern confuses the predator trying to get close to the actual eggs. These frogs have even been known to kick away predatory wasps.

In Real Life

If you kiss a common frog, no prince will appear, as it did in the fairy-tale *The Frog Prince*. Instead, you will get a slimy feel and a bad infection because frogs are known to carry bacteria called 'Salmonella'. Never try touching a wild frog or a toad; you never know what toxins they might carry!

Smooth-sided Toad

Smooth-sided toads are medium-sized animals. The skin of the toad is spotted and brown. This acts as a camouflage, making it easy for the toad to hide on the forest floor. The smooth appearance is deceptive, as the warty skin with toxin glands is present in these toads as well, it is just not as obvious.

The smooth-sided toad has warts behind its eyes called the parotid glands. These produce dangerous toxins which can interfere with the predator's heart, even leading to death sometimes.

It is seen in the rainforests of countries such as Brazil, Colombia, Guyana, Ecuador, Suriname, and Venezuela. The animal can remain active all through the day and night and eats mostly insects.

▲ Smooth-sided toads are relatively sooth compared to the thicker, bumpier, and dry skins of most toads

Sign of Warning

An oriental fire-bellied toad looks like a regular toad with black spots covering its green skin. It blends well with the leaves and trees found in its habitats located in China, Korea, parts of Japan, and southern Russia.

The toad has a secret weapon; its skin secretes toxins. When it feels threatened, it rolls on its back and reveals its black and red underside, as it wants to warn the predator about the effects of eating it. In other words, it tries to tell the predator to stay away or it might die due to poisoning.

Incredible Individuals

A herpetologist is a person who studies amphibians and reptiles. Ross Allen was a famous herpetologist, born in the USA. He developed anti-venoms after studying snakes. He also handled the animals used in movies such as *Tarzan Finds a Son*.

▼ The oriental fire-bellied toad lives in ponds and streams

Turtle or Tortoise?

Are you confused about which is which? All tortoises are turtles, but not all turtles are tortoises! To make it simpler, 'turtle' is the broad name used for any animal which belongs to order Testudinata. Apart from a few structural differences between turtles and tortoises, the easiest way to differentiate between the two is the habitat that they are adapted to. Tortoises aren't adapted to water.

The Turtle Checklist

You know it is a turtle if:

✔ It lives in water. Some turtles live in freshwater, some in saltwater and some are amphibious, that is, they live both on land and in water;

✔ It is an omnivore, eating both plants and animals;

✔ It has a flattened and streamlined dome, allowing it to easily swim in water;

✔ It is aquatic or amphibious. Turtles have webbed feet which aid swimming. It is only the sea turtles which have proper flippers, which they use to swim long distances in the ocean.

▲ Unlike most turtles, the Eastern box turtle has a dome-shaped shell

The Tortoise Checklist

You know it is a tortoise if:

✔ It is a terrestrial animal;

✔ It eats plants; though, there are a few varieties living in humid forest regions which are known to consume flesh and other insects;

✔ It has a large, high, dome-like shell. Unless it is the pancake tortoise that lives in Kenya, Tanzania and Zimbabwe. The pancake tortoise has a softer, more flat shell which helps it squeeze between rocks;

✔ It has stalky hind legs like an elephant's, designed to aid walking on land.

▲ A sea turtle gliding through water using its flippers

▲ Gopher tortoises use their legs to make burrows as deep as 10 feet into the ground

Isn't It Amazing!

The turtle is considered to be a sign of good luck in many cultures across the world. In India, the tortoise or 'kurma' in Sanskrit, is supposed to be the second incarnation of Lord Vishnu. Ancient Egyptians wore amulets depicting turtles as they believed this would keep them healthy. Turtles were also considered as the enemy of Ra, or Re, who was the Sun God.

Story of the Neck

Turtles are divided into two groups depending on how they tuck their necks inside their shells. The hidden-necked turtles can hide their heads completely inside their shells, while the side-necked turtles can turn their heads to one side and hide them just under the edge of their shells. Turtles or tortoises usually hide their heads for protection against any threats in the environment.

◀ The matamata turtle from South America can turn its head to one side

◀ A mud turtle with its head hidden inside its shell

Alike but Unlike

Can you tell a crocodile and an alligator apart? How about a worm lizard and a small snake? Scientists might have divided reptiles into orders, species and even families in bigger classifications, but there are a few animals which look so similar that it is difficult to make out who's who. So, let's learn to differentiate between these species.

Cousins

Alligators and crocodiles belong to order Crocodilia. So, if you want to refer to them as a group, you say 'crocodilians' but the word 'crocodile' isn't as inclusive.

Both are large, toothy predators, with long snouts, armours on their backs, and powerful tails. At a glance, they look so alike that it is hard to tell the difference between them. But here is how they are different from each other:

- Alligators have a wide head with the snout rounded into a U-shape, while crocodiles have narrow heads with snouts ending in sharp V-shapes.
- Both have one large tooth on the lower jaw. In the case of alligators, the tooth fits into a pit of the upper jaw and is not visible when the mouth is shut. However, in crocodiles, the tooth fits into a notch in the upper jaw but is still visible when the mouth is shut.
- Alligators are usually grey or black, while crocodiles are mostly olive or a pale brown in colour.
- Alligators prefer to live in freshwater, while crocodiles tend to be comfortable in saltwater.

▲ An American alligator, also called the Alligator mississipiensis, at the edge of a freshwater lake

In Real Life

There are only two species in the genus Alligator—the American alligator, which is found throughout the southeastern coast of the USA, and the critically endangered Chinese alligator that lives in the Anhui province of China.

▶ The Nile crocodile, Africa's largest crocodile, is a menacing maneater

Crawling Crocodilians

While on the one hand crocodilians are ruthless killers, they also fiercely guard their young ones. They live by the riverbanks and are among the most endangered species in the world. Their dwindling numbers are a result of global warming and human activity.

Gharials

Also called gavials, they have long, thin snouts and are mainly found in Asia. Their numbers are so low that the gharial has been declared as a critically endangered species by the International Union of Conservation of Nature (IUCN).

A Vanishing Home

Once upon a time, this reptile was found in abundance in countries like India, Pakistan, Nepal, and Myanmar. Today, it can only be found in India along the Son, Chambal, and Girwa rivers; and in Nepal, along the Narayani River.

What caused this decline? Around 98 per cent of the gharial population was lost to hunting for use in traditional medicine. Also, human beings have changed the courses of rivers to suit their needs. This has dried up many riverbeds, which were home to these precious reptiles.

A Pot for a Name

The males of these species have a bulb-like growth on their long snout, which resembles a *'ghara'*, which in Hindi means 'pot'; that is why this reptile is called 'gharial'. Males use these bulbous growths to call out and blow bubbles during the mating season to attract mates.

▼ *Not only are gharials critically endangered, but their population is also declining*

What Do They Look Like?

An adult gharial is close to almost 907 kilograms and can be 12–15 feet in length. Males are usually larger than females. These reptiles have weak legs and adults are unable to raise their bodies once on land. The long snout has sensory cells which detect vibrations created in water. The reptile, on sensing these vibrations, moves its head from side to side with force and tracks down the prey. It then grabs it firmly in its jaw, which has more than a hundred teeth. Adults mostly eat fish; however, young gharials are seen eating invertebrates found in the waters.

▲ *A giant gharial with a long snout*

The Creation

Gharials usually mate in the dry season. The female lays eggs near slow-moving water around the riverbank, where she digs a hole to lay eggs. Unlike many other reptiles, she does not leave the nest unguarded.
The eggs hatch in about 70 days and the hatchlings stay with their mother for weeks or even months, until they are ready to survive on their own.

We Are Crocodilians Too

Caimans are several species of reptiles belonging to the Crocodilian family. They are found in Central and South America. These are carnivores, living along the riverbanks or any other type of water bodies such as ponds or lakes. Like others in the order, they lay eggs, build nests and guard their young ones.

The spectacled caiman, as the name suggests, has a bony ridge between its eyes that looks like the nosepiece of an eyeglass. This reptile has made its home in an area between southern Mexico and Brazil.

▼ Caimans are also called caymans. They were once sold to people as pets

◄ At night, when light is shown on them, the spectacled caiman's eyes reflect red light, making it easy to spot them in the dark

The Yacare caiman is found in central parts of South America. It loves to feast on piranhas. About three decades ago, it was at the brink of extinction, thanks to armed gangs which killed them for their skin. The Brazilian government banned poaching, raising their numbers to almost ten million today.

Talking Eggs

Did you know crocodile eggs can get noisy just before hatching? When the babies are fully grown inside the egg, they call out to their siblings, telling them it is time to hatch; and to their mother, asking her to uncover the nest.

The Loving Crocodiles

They might be ferocious otherwise, but female crocodiles are gentle, caring mothers. Not only do they care for the eggs, but when they hatch, the mothers carry the newborn in their jaws into the water. If the mother hears a call of distress from her child, she rushes to the rescue. She also calls out to them when she wants them to assemble around her.

► Crocodiles lay 10–60 eggs at a time

◄ The mother crocodile does not shut her jaw, because it might hurt her babies

Stealthy Hunters

All crocodilians have a knack for hunting. They lurk underwater, with just their eyes and nostrils peeping above the surface. They can be as still as a log for hours together. Relying on their excellent eyesight, the moment they spot a prey, they swim over and catch it in their jaws in a matter of seconds.

In Real Life

Crocodiles, alligators, caimans, and gharials are famous for their precious skin which is converted to bags, belts, and other items. Crocodile meat is also considered to be a delicacy in parts of the world. Most countries have banned the killing of these animals in the wild, yet poachers lurk as the skin and meat get a huge price in international markets.

▲ A caiman hiding underwater

The World of Snakes

You know a snake when you see it. The animal is covered with overlapping scales. Larger ones protect the reptile's belly. These horizontally arranged scales enhance the snake's ability to slide on the ground or climb up a tree. Snakes shed their outer layer of skin in a process called **moulting**. The colours and patterns of snakeskin vary from one species to another.

The Mouth

Did you know a snake's mouth can open really wide? They have a special jaw that allows them to swallow whole a prey much larger than their size. It is the forked tongue of the snake which picks up the smell. It picks up chemical molecules from the surroundings and sends information to a special organ called Jacobson's organ, situated in the head. Here, the information is processed, and it helps the snake track down its prey.

▲ *The forked tongue gives snakes a more acute and directional sense of smell*

The Teeth

All snakes bite, but few are venomous. The word venom means poison. Some snakes have two fangs. These are long, narrow, hollow teeth that lie flat against the roof of the snake's mouth, but the moment a snake sinks its fangs into a prey, muscular pressure releases the venom from a gland located near the eyes. This venom either mobilises the prey or kills it.

▶ *A snake baring its fangs*

Are all Venomous Snakes Lethal?

Venomous snakes are smart because they do not waste venom on objects they cannot prey on. That is why, although there are about 300 species of venomous snakes, only half are capable of causing lethal harm to human beings. In most cases the human beings are bit in defence as the snake feels that the human being in question is a threat.

Teeth with Another Tale

The non-venomous snakes usually have small sharp teeth which curve backwards. The snake uses these teeth to latch onto a prey, not allowing it to escape as the snake wraps its muscular body around it. Many snakes grow more teeth than required, as some are lost while biting and feeding.

Snake Hug

Most non-venomous snakes and a few venomous ones use constriction as a method to kill their prey. They coil around the prey and suffocate it to death.

▲ *A snake coiled around a rat*

Incredible Individuals

Anti-venom is a substance used to treat snake bites against the venom of a particular species of snakes. The first anti-venom was created by Albert Calmette, a scientist working with the Pasteur Institute. It was made against the venom of the Indian cobra, scientifically known as *Naja Naja*.

A King Among Snakes

King cobras are not just one of the most venomous snakes in the world; they can literally 'stand' and rise to the height of a human being. These snakes are found in India, southern China, and Southeast Asia.

Appearance

King cobras, slender in body, are an average of 12 feet in length, but can reach almost 18 feet. The prominent feature of this species is the presence of 11 large scales on the top of its head. It comes in varied colours and can be black, brown, yellow, or olive green.

The snake's back has crossbar-like sections in white or yellow, while the underside can be monochromatic, with or without the embellishment of bars. The area near the throat is usually light yellow or a brownish cream colour.

◀ *The common stance of a king cobra*

Hunters

King cobras live in forests, fields, and even villages. They can move around at night and in the day time. They are not just seen on land, but also on trees, and in water. They feed on small mammals, bird's eggs, lizards, and even venomous and non-venomous snakes.

Attackers

King cobras do not attack unless they feel threatened. They start out with a loud hiss and spread out their hoods. If the threat persists, they bite. They may not be the most venomous snakes in the world, but the amount of venom they inject into a single bite is enough to kill not just an elephant but almost twenty adult human beings.

Prey

Human beings have killed so many king cobras for medicine, leather, as well as for entertainment, or in the name of religion, that the poor animal is now on the IUCN list of threatened species.

Nesting

On mating, the female of the species lays eggs in a nest. These are the only snakes in the world which don't just build nests but guard them as well. The nest is built by the female using soil, dead leaves, and other buildable materials that she finds on the ground. She coils herself into an arm-like stance to build the nest.

In the Waters

69 species of snakes abound the warm coastal waters of the Pacific and Indian Oceans. However, the span of the yellow-bellied sea snake is much wider, reaching waters of the west coasts of both South and North America.

▲ *Yellow-bellied sea snakes have the greatest territory expanse amongst all sea snakes*

Traits

Yellow-bellied sea snakes have flat bodies with oar-like tails and small scales on the back. In a few species, the belly scales are almost absent, making crawling on land impossible for them. They lead most of their lives in water and have elongated lungs almost as long as their bodies.

The sea snakes are known for breathing through the skin. This helps them stay under water for long hours. However, as they have to reach the sea floor for food, they tend to stay in shallow waters, not deeper than 100 feet. They feed on a variety of fish as well as eels.

The Giant of Galapagos

The Galapagos islands can be found in the Pacific Ocean, around 1,000 kilometres off the coast of South America. This network of 19 volcanic islands is home to many rare species of animals. One such species is the giant tortoise or Galapagos tortoise. They are among the longest living vertebrate animals in the world, with an average lifespan of 100 years!

Brief History

The Galapagos Islands were discovered in 1535 by a man named Tomas de Berlanga, who was the bishop of Panama, while travelling to Peru. He saw many tortoises there and named the islands after them, since the Spanish word for these animals is galapagos.

It became famous after many other explorers and even pirates visited the islands. Eventually, it caught the attention of Charles Darwin, who visited the islands in 1835. He encountered almost 15 types of giant tortoises and made a series of observations, which have helped conservationists understand these animals better.

Darwin's Observations

The giant tortoise weighs almost 215 kilograms and is close to 4 feet in length. The tortoise meat was eaten by the inhabitants of the islands and even Charles Darwin tasted it. Island inhabitants would spend around two days hunting a tortoise, but would get enough meat to last them a week! Darwin took home three tortoises for observation.

▼ *Born back in 1832, Jonathan, the oldest living giant tortoise could be 189 years old*

The Shell

The shell of a tortoise is a part of its skeleton. The curved upper part is called the carapace and is supported by the backbone. The lower part, the **plastron**, protects the belly of the animal. The shells are made up of hard bony material, which is covered by a layer of keratin. The shells of the Galapagos tortoises are divided into two types.

The Dome Shell

The dome-shelled tortoises have carapaces angled in such a way that it restricts the extent to which the animal can raise its head. These types tend to live on humid Galapagos islands with abundant vegetation, making it easier to eat food.

Saddle-shaped Shell

The animals with saddle-shaped shells live on the hotter and drier islands of Galapagos. To survive, their carapaces are angled in such a way, that they can stretch their heads to reach out to vegetation hanging high up.

To Stand and Stare

Galapagos tortoises lead laid-back lives. They bask in the Sun and nap for almost 16 hours a day. The tortoises that live in humid areas eat grass, leaves, and berries. On the other hand, the ones that live in drier regions tend to feed on succulent cactus leaves. They enjoy bathing in water, but can go without food or water for almost a year as they have a slow **metabolism** and massive internal water stores.

Incredible Individuals

Charles Darwin developed his theory of evolution on the Galapagos islands. He had come to the islands after joining the *HMS Beagle*. The commander of the ship had decided to take along people who would explore the islands and the 22-year-old Darwin had accepted the opportunity.

▲ Charles Darwin

Before the journey, Darwin was a student at Cambridge, first studying medicine and then divinity. However, his disinterest in his studies embarrassed his father. It was only when Darwin informally studied geology that something sparked within him.

◀ Male tortoises might stretch out their necks and bite each other to show dominance

Breeding

During the breeding season, between January to June, males make roaring noises. Females never use their voice. The female lays between 2 to 20 eggs that resemble a tennis ball in size. She digs a hole for the eggs with her hind feet. Once the eggs are covered, she leaves. The eggs hatch after four to eight months, from November to April. The hatchlings are on their own right from the beginning.

Survival

Since Darwin left the islands, the number of the giant tortoises has come down to 10. An estimated 100,000 tortoises have been killed for food in the last 300 years. The main natural predator of the eggs and the hatchlings is the Galapagos hawk. But in case of adult tortoises, illegal hunting and destruction of habitats have made these animals vulnerable to extinction. Conservation efforts by the Charles Darwin Research Centre, under which the eggs and hatchlings are kept in captivity to be released at the right time, are turning out to be helpful.

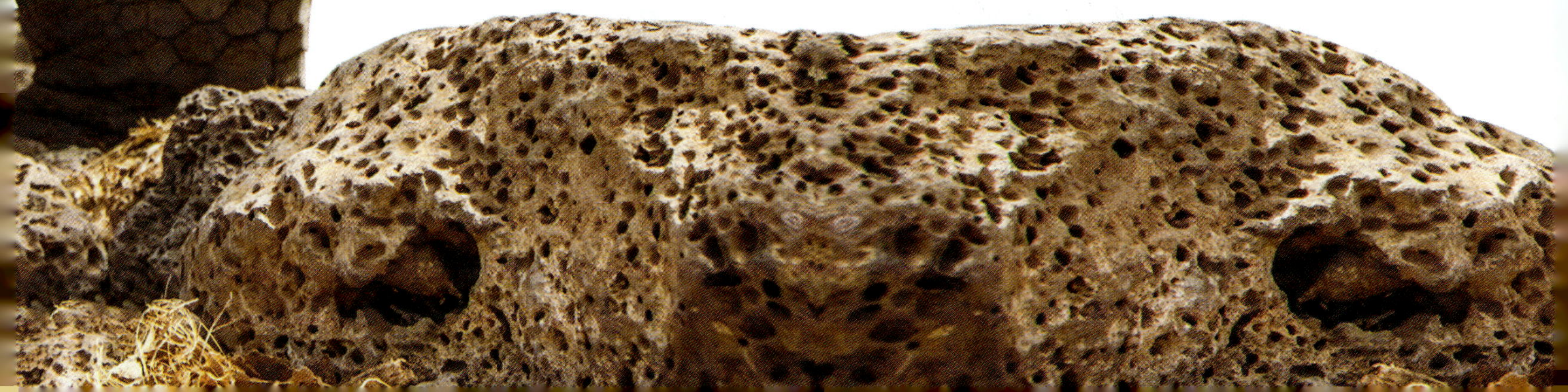

Sensitive Amphibians

Amphibians partially breathe through their skin. This makes them sensitive to radiation, acid rain, ozone depletion, habitat destruction, pollution, and climatic changes. This is why amphibians are also considered to be indicators of environmental changes.

Playing a Host of Roles

There have been many notions surrounding frogs. Medieval Europeans believed them to be devils. Ancient Egyptians believed that frogs were a symbol of fertility and life. Many children have learned to dissect frogs in their biology classrooms. To scientists, they are a species that have survived millions of years. They are an essential part of the fragile ecosystems of Earth, a prey at times and predator at others. Life without them is impossible!

In the Face of Mass Extinction

Various species of frogs, toads, newts, salamanders, and other amphibians are under threat of extinction because of climatic changes. An example of this is the Chinese giant salamander which has been listed as critically endangered according to the IUCN list. This is because it fills many dinner plates. Yes, because of exploitation for food, there are just a handful of these animals surviving in the wild. The Malagasy rainbow frog that lives in Madagascar too is threatened by the global pet trade.

▲ There are five recognised species of the giant salamander

Fungal Destruction

High in California's Sierra Nevada, the mountain yellow-legged frogs are dying in big numbers. The reason is amphibian chytrid fungus. It first appeared in 2004 and has killed thousands of animals since then.

The fungus attacks the protein in the amphibian's skin and mouth. This could negatively impact the exchange of gases and the balance of electrolytes, both of which are vital for survival.

▲ Sierra Nevada mountain yellow-legged frog on a granite rock in the water

▶ This is the Lehmann's poison frog. It is found in the Colombian jungles of South America. Logging and land development for agriculture has made it critically endangered

▼ The Panamanian golden frog is extinct in the wild. A huge population of this frog has been killed because of the chytrid fungus

Species under Threat

There are many species under threat today, but the Kihansi spray toad and the Panamanian golden frog are some disturbing examples.

▶ The Kihansi spray toad, as the name suggests, lives amidst the spray of Kihansi and Mhalala waterfalls in the Udzungwa mountains in Tanzania. It is critically endangered

▶ Black mambas are adapted to live both on the ground and on trees, which they climb easily

The Venomous Black Mamba

Snakes that can inject venom into their prey are called venomous snakes. Some snakes can also harm human beings with their venom. The substance is poisonous and dangerous. Anti-venom is the cure for venom. Scientists have come up with several anti-venoms by studying snakes and experimenting with their venom.

Black Mamba

The black mamba is considered to be one of the deadliest snakes of Africa. It is found in the grassy areas and hills of the continent's southern and eastern parts. It is a quick, aggressive, and extremely venomous snake.

The black mamba is not black in colour. It is actually brown! But it gets its name from the blue-black colour found inside its mouth, which it opens wide when threatened. It is Africa's longest venomous snake, reaching almost up to 9 feet in length on an average. It is also one of the fastest snakes in the world and can move at a speed of 20 kmph.

For its aggressive nature, the black mamba is shy. It prefers escape to confrontation. However, if it does feel threatened, it may raise its body to almost one-third of its length and open its mouth to let out a loud hiss. The snake shows its true colours if the threat persists. It attacks multiple times with its fangs, injecting its lethal venom each time.

Potent Venom

Black mamba's venom is a **neurotoxin** that paralyses the prey, killing it eventually. If the human beings who are bit do not get the anti-venom immediately, they might die within 20 minutes of the attack. Every year it is responsible for numerous deaths in its home ground, however, some legends and rumours falsely exaggerate these numbers even more.

It is possible that the legends were influenced by the fact that in many rural areas where the black mamba strikes, the **antidote** is not still easily available. Interestingly, recent research shows that black-mamba venom could be more effective than morphine as a painkiller.

This snake is usually found near termite hills. It is either here or in tree hollows that it lays its eggs. It feeds on small mammals and birds.

▲ The brown colour of the black mamba helps the snake camouflage in its surroundings

Isn't It Amazing!

India is often associated with snake charmers. While it is wrong and offensive to stereotype a country in such a way, snake charmers do exist and offer their services as entertainment. They play music and pretend that the snake is dancing to their tune, though in reality, snakes cannot hear very well. The snake charmers are often semi-nomadic and carry king cobras with them. They never harm the animal since it is their source of livelihood. So, if a snake enters a home in a village, they might be the first to be called to remove it.

Activate Defence Mode

Reptiles and amphibians aggressively prey on animals and defend themselves with ease. Many small reptiles fall prey to carnivorous birds, mammals, and even larger reptiles. To protect themselves from danger, small reptiles such as lizards, snakes, and turtles have devised interesting methods of defence. Similarly, amphibians also have special adaptations that keep them safe.

Ball Up!

The armadillo girdled lizard is found in South Africa. This animal has a unique method of defence. The moment it senses danger, it curls its body into the shape of a ball by holding its tail in its mouth. For attackers, such as snakes, it becomes difficult to swallow the armadillo girdled lizard, not just because they do not know how to take the ball into their mouth, but also because it has a hard, bony covering, and a spiny tail and head. The lizard remains in this shape till the danger passes.

▶ An armadillo girdled lizard in the defence pose

A Frilled Fight

The Australian frilled lizard uses many tactics to scare off its predators, such as opening its mouth wide, which causes the skin flap to open on both sides of its mouth, making it appear like the lizard has a frilled collar. It also lashes its tail back and forth and makes hissing sounds.

▲ The Australian frilled lizards are threatened by birds, dingoes, and snakes

The Mimic

Scarlet kingsnakes are a smart variety. As part of a defence mechanism called 'mimicry', these harmless snakes sport bright colours similar to the venomous coral snake. Seeing the colours, predators mistake them for the dangerous coral snakes and stay away.

▲ These snakes are around 30 to 50 centimetres in length

Hognose

Hognose snakes feign death if threatened. They roll on their backsides and hang their mouths open. They also emit smells similar to decaying flesh. The predator believes that the snake has been poisoned or diseased and moves away.

◀ Hognose snakes are found in North and South America

In Real Life

Hognose snakes have mild venom, but they are not constrictors. They swallow their prey (like toads) whole. Their venom is not toxic to human beings. They tend to be relatively calm and do not bite trainers. Hognose snakes are shy, so their first defence is to hide from their predators. They hide in burrows or leaves. They are often taken captive and are easy to care for.

Hinge-back Tortoise

Apart from stiff, bony shells which are the first line of defence in tortoises, few species also have hinges on the shell. When threatened, the hinges allow the front and back of the animal to close tightly, protecting its soft body parts. Not just this, the hinges also give a painful pinch to the predator.

Incredible Individuals

In Malaysia, there was a famous snake charmer named Ali Khan Samsuddin. He was nicknamed 'King of the Snakes'. Often during his exhilarating shows, he was seen kissing snakes like the king cobra. He once lived in a glass cage with 400 snakes for 40 days. When he was 21, he was first bit by a king cobra but survived. Then again at the age of 48, he was bit by another king cobra, leading to his demise.

▲ *The hinge-back tortoise likes to look for water underground by burying its head into the land when the water is sparse*

A Horned Defence

Thorny devils are adapted to the Australian outback heat. They have moisture-attracting grooves between the scales. During nights, when dew condenses on their bodies, the grooves take in the moisture and send it to the mouth. This helps them survive harsh climates.

These lizards have prickly horns protruding from their skin. They protect the lizard from being eaten, as the predator stays away seeing the horns. If this does not work, they squirt out blood from tiny vessels near their eyes to scare off the attacker.

▲ *Thorny devils survive on ants*

Common Snapping Turtle

Common snapping turtles often remain buried in muddied shallow waters. They are not aggressive in water, but on land they move forcefully towards the attacker and try snapping their mouths aggressively.

▲ *Do not be fooled by its appearance, a turtle can have a sharp bite*

Five-lined Skink

The five-lined skink wriggles its tail to distract predators. The vertebrae of their tails have special fracture points. If pulled from these points, the tail falls off. The attacker's attention goes to the still-wriggling tail. It lets the lizard out of its mouth and makes a grab for the tail. The lizard escapes and eventually grows a new tail.

▼ *These lizards have grey, brown or black skin*

Home Is Where the Habitat Is

Almost all organisms on this planet have homes. There are places that reptiles and amphibians inhabit because they suit their lifestyles the best. These habitats provide them with food, water, and shelter as per their needs. Reptiles and amphibians populate the many places marked on the map below, where they share their homes with other animals.

🐾 Amazon Rainforest (South America)

The Amazon River is home to one of the last surviving rainforests in the world. It has abundant trees, swamps, rivulets, and streams for amphibians to live comfortably.

There are many varieties of frogs in the Amazon River. The giant cane toad is a large species that has made its home here. Its skin secretes a toxin so potent that if a cat or dog holds it in its mouth, the animal will die.

▲ *The largest cane toad was 53.9 centimetres long when stretched from snout to tail, and weighed 2.65 kilograms*

🐾 Western Ghats (India)

Western Ghats lie over the long western coastline of India. They are an ecological treat and are considered one of the eight 'hotspots' of biological diversity around the world. The area is home to at least 325 varieties of threatened plants, mammals, fish, amphibians, and birds.

New species are often discovered here. In 2016, two new species of leaping frogs were discovered here. One is *Indirana paramakri*; it was found on wet rocks and leaves near streams in Kerala. The species is reddish brown with a distinctive snout and unique toe webbing. The other one, *Indirana bhadrai*, is light brown.

▲ *Western Ghats*

🐾 Everglades (USA)

Also called the 'Big Swamp', the Everglades are wetlands of Florida. They are a World Heritage Site. The Everglades are also called the 'river of grass', because of unending miles of sawgrass, at times so thick that one forgets there is water beneath, or '*pahayokee*' (grassy water), as it is called by the Native Americans.

▲ *The grassy waters of the Everglades*

Snake Island (Brazil)

Off the coast of the city of Sao Paulo lies an island which could be considered the deadliest island in the world. Scientists estimate that around 4,000 snakes inhabit this tiny island. No wonder it is called so.

Here resides the golden lancehead viper, considered to be one of the most venomous pit vipers in the world. Its venom is supposed to be more potent than that of any mainland species.

How was this deadly island created? Once upon a time, it was attached to mainland Brazil, but rising sea levels separated it from the mainland. The snakes there were able to multiply because of the lack of any ground predators.

▲ Snake Island is called Ilha de Queimada Grande

▶ Behold the deadly and toxic golden lancehead viper

▲ Hell Creek is sometimes referred to as 'badlands' because it is barren, eroded, and almost devoid of vegetation

Hell Creek Formation (USA)

The first-ever *Tyrannosaurus rex* fossil was discovered in 1902 by a palaeontologist named Barnum Brown at Hell Creek Formation in Montana. The fossil belonged to the Cretaceous Age, about 75 million years ago. Since then, several fossils of various dinosaurs have been discovered in this area. To name a few, we have the *Triceratops*, *Edmontosaurus* and *Ankylosaurus*. The entire region was a wet swampy land where dinosaurs roamed freely. To really experience the region's bounty, one can take part in excavation programmes at Hell Creek! All we need is a guide, a digging supervisor and a calm mind to make sure no fossil is damaged in the process.

Madagascar (Africa)

The island of Madagascar is not just home to the world's smallest chameleon, but also to the world's longest, the Parson's chameleon. This reptile can grow almost up to 70 centimetres in length. If you want to see this lizard, you will have to make a trip to the rainforests on the island. These chameleons live on trees there.

They have independently moving eyes and a triangular head similar to other types of chameleons. A long tail is used for gripping branches. The chameleon's long, sticky tongue helps it capture insects.

Odisha (India)

Olive ridley turtles are found in warm waters of the three oceans, the Atlantic, Pacific, and Indian. They are named so because of the greenish colour of their skin and carapace. These reptiles are small, measuring about 2 feet in length.

The female turtles migrate thousands of kilometres to lay eggs. One such site is the coastline of Odisha in India. Females visit it in large numbers, making it a mass nesting site.

▲ To ensure that some will hatch, live, and make it to adulthood, they lay 120–150 eggs at a time!

Like most chameleons, Parson's too changes colour not just as camouflage, but also based on environmental factors such as light and temperature, as well as based on the presence of other chameleons.

▶ Parson's chameleons are said to be gentle lizards

Word check

Amphibians: It is a class of animals that are cold-blooded and includes vertebrates such as frogs, toads, newts, salamanders and caecilians. All amphibians are aquatic at the larval stage and have gills. They metamorphise into adults who can move on land and breathe using lungs.

Antidote: It is the medicine given to nullify the effects of poison.

Arthropods: It is a class of invertebrate animals that have an exoskeleton, a segmented body, and paired appendages that are jointed. They are a very diverse group, with around 10 million species worldwide, such as lobsters, spiders, centipedes, many types of insects.

Exoskeleton: It is the hard, external covering seen in invertebrate animals.

Larva: It is a stage in the life of an amphibian or insect where it is completely different from its adult form.

Lobe-finned fish: These fish have a central appendage made up of bones and cartilage in their fins. This is what helped tetrapods walk on land.

Mesozoic Era: It was a period around 65 million years ago when giant dinosaurs, birds and reptiles dominated Earth.

Metabolism: It refers to the chemical reactions that take place within the body of an animal, including digestion and respiration.

Moulting: It is the process by which an animal sheds its exoskeleton and grows another.

Neurotoxin: It is a type of venom that paralyses or stuns the prey.

Plastron: It is the underside of a tortoise or turtle's shell.

Sauropsids: It is a group of amniotic animals that consists of birds and reptiles.

Synapsids: It is the class of animals containing all mammal species.

Tetrapod: It is an animal that possesses four feet.

Triassic takeover: It lasted between 251 and 199 million years ago after the Permian Mass Extinction wiped out most synapsids and sauropsids began to evolve.